Glass City Blues

poems by

Nathan Elias

Finishing Line Press
Georgetown, Kentucky

Glass City Blues

Copyright © 2018 by Nathan Elias
ISBN 978-1-63534-691-6 First Edition
All rights reserved under International and Pan-American Copyright Conventions.
No part of this book may be reproduced in any manner whatsoever without written permission from the publisher, except in the case of brief quotations embodied in critical articles and reviews.

ACKNOWLEDGMENTS

Many thanks to the editors of the publications in which these poems previously appeared:

Red Fez: "Glass City Blues", "Throwing Rocks at Cars, 1996", "Flight of the Soul", "The Untamed Heart"
the beatnik: "Glass City Blues" (Reprint)
The Mill: "The Burning Valley Midwest Twenty-Three"
Literary Orphans: "The Burning Valley Midwest Twenty-Three" (Reprint)
Rust + Moth: "Ghost of a Toledo Girl"
Philosophical Idiot: "Urn", "There Are Nights I Lie"
Stonecoast Review: "Night Ride along the River"
Cacti Fur: "Level Three Emergency"
Drunk in a Midnight Choir: "Aboard the Sunset Limited", "Cutter's Remorse"
The Literary Nest: "Playing Your Old Guitar on the Fourth of July"
The Capstone Review: "if you want a revolution"
Poems for All: "Body Work", "Silver Halide"
The Literary Yard: "The Cliffs of Palos Verdes"
Drunk Monkeys: "A Shallow Argument at Venice Beach"
After the Pause: "Forgotten Love Songs", "Sometime, Somewhere", "We Made Love and Dyed Your Hair Purple"
Spry Literary Journal: "Learning to Drown"

Publisher: Leah Maines
Editor: Christen Kincaid
Cover Art and Design: Alexi Milano
Author Photo: Alexi Milano

Printed in the USA on acid-free paper.
Order online: www.finishinglinepress.com
      also available on amazon.com

              Author inquiries and mail orders:
                    Finishing Line Press
                      P. O. Box 1626
                Georgetown, Kentucky 40324
                         U. S. A.

Table of Contents

Part One: Glass City Blues

Glass City Blues 1
The Burning Valley Midwest Twenty-Three 2
Urn 3
Ghost of a Toledo Girl... 4
Cutter's Remorse... 5
Night Ride along the River 6
Learning to Drown 7
Throwing Rocks at Cars, 1996 8
The Rabbit Wringer.. 9
Level Three Emergency... 10
Body Work 11

Part Two: How to Build a Heart

Forgotten Love Songs.. 13
We Made Love and Dyed Your Hair Purple 14
Flight of the Soul 15
Sometime, Somewhere 16
The Untamed Heart.. 17

Part Three: From Los Angeles with Love

Silver Halide 19
A Shallow Argument at Venice Beach 20
There Are Nights I Lie.. 21
Playing Your Old Guitar on the Fourth of July.................. 22
if you want a revolution 23
Blind Alto Midnight... 24
The Cliffs of Palos Verdes 25
Aboard the Sunset Limited 26

PART ONE

GLASS

CITY

BLUES

Glass City Blues

The night begins on the river bottom,
slow dancing again with a lover's ghost.
We light a cigarette and call for the sax
to play a tune that will bury the dead.

It's happy hour and sorrow
is on tap. Two rounds before we're on stage
singing, *but for me there can be no dawn*
I thought I was in paradise.

Moonlight guides our feet as we
move to the sound of piano keys on fire,
the black cat trumpet, the ambulance
crescendo of Glass City blues.

We break the surface of air
like hard-boiled eggs then choke it down
with rose water. I am between the teeth
of stray dogs in a street fight

and if this is another dream
I'll count bullets and graves before
I search for her in the pouring rain, trying
to remember what her mother named her.

The Burning Valley Midwest Twenty-Three

I felt the fire's rock-steady inertia pulling us along,
through smoky clouds overlooking the glass ghost valley.
We rose where rivers intersect at the wrist like vapor
null to the sound of history's heavy heartbeat.

We burned and crowed in harmony with rusty
road-show record players, rocked forth and back, lost
and high on the frequency of rickshaw radio, got lit
off those soothsayer poets, bohemian angels

whose albino guise danced the Macarena
under pale blue Boricua moonlight and led
our mariachi band to a sky where gravity sang
the violin verses of underwater maestros,

whose bloody feet fled the West Palm wasteland
after Los Angeles, after Philadelphia, after the Black
Swamp to chase down the last hellhounds in waking
madness, in the shadow of tombstone fields

where the writing thousands revived
Darwin and reminded the five-sided figures
to burn inside the church of time, inhale
paraffin breath from spitfire lungs.

All at once they opened their mouths, lit up
the midnight valley of the Midwest muse and cast
lonesome pavonian fireworks down the throat
where the bones and belly still cry for life.

Urn

I've come for the ashes.

I've come to bury
snapdragon
seeds.

I've come to put to rest
a decade,   dialysis.

In a North Toledo bar, they serve breakfast
on Christmas and we feast
like it's your last meal.

You always make me
promise to scatter her somewhere
beautiful. You've held on too
long; the time has come
to bind and release
us both.

Ghost of a Toledo Girl

At 16 I couldn't get Kurt Cobain's name
tattooed across my chest, so I stitched
patches of my favorite bands onto a sweater
and wore it like armor to protect my heart.

Mom's shotgun only made the myth
more real, death a fairy tale about escape.
In a city made of mirrors, I saw
nothing but infinite misery.

From the other side, I cannot weep
for my mother or myself, but I can sing
loud enough to shatter glass, hoping
she will hear me and forgive.

I search for what cannot live or die,
like music, or emotion—me at my last
concert with a broken, bloody nose,
smiling without a care.

Cutter's Remorse

Cigarette burns, finger-length
scars won't disappear.

As a butcher's apprentice
I learned to grind bone and slice
away the animal.

Night Ride along the River

I dug up
the two keys you buried
in our backyard—
a tin box
with bullets,
your name

inscribed across the top
like on a tombstone.
A note inside
said, "Son,
do not use
until after
I am gone."

On an August sunset,
I opened the old shed
with one key, started
your motorcycle
with the other.

I revved
the engine like you
taught me that Thanksgiving
we started talking again.

I could have died,
coasting down
River Road,
firing your gun
at the sky,
but somehow
I knew you
wouldn't
let me
fall.

Learning to Drown

The lake, its muddy hands tighten
around my neck, wrestle the life out
of my flooded bed. A ghost, feeding
on lichen, I've become another

water-logged body, dancing in slow-motion
as the world glimmers with refracted light.
What have I left behind on the surface
where memory fishes my remains,

its hook a rusted minute-hand
ready to pull me from this blue dream?
The lake, its seaweed lips whisper
lullabies in a gurgling language

as sleep consumes my lungs.
Beneath this aquatic tomb, I wait for air
to fill me and morning to emerge again.

Throwing Rocks at Cars, 1996
for Ben

You put limestone in my hand
and say *on the count of three.*
I have seen you paint cement
with people's kneecaps. You
are fluent in the language of
hooded crows, of broken bones.
In eleven years, you will be launched
through a windshield, and the cushion
of your body will be the only thing
to prevent the death of your
sweetheart. Three.

The Rabbit Wringer

My hot finger grips the trigger
of my father's .410 single-barrel shotgun.
He tells me to be silent and wait for the rabbit
to reveal itself on the white forest carpet.

Keep your eyes open, he says,
and be cautious of movement
because if you miss that rabbit run
there will be no kill.

Clouds of breath indicate life
hiding in nature's last winter shadow.
The gun in my hand does not tremble,
preserved like these petrified woods.

It shows itself, little heart racing
across a plate of white—I shoot
and leave a trail of blood
in its footprints.

Level Three Emergency

We're snowed in
at a Motel 6
and I've still got it,
the gold chain we stole
from your mother
that rainy Easter.

Tell me to turn up the radio
and dance like we'll die here,
frozen and hungry, naked.
There is no resisting fire.

I could last forever, a jewel
thief for you, searching
for enough amber
to fossilize our love.

Tell me to wear this gold
chain around my neck, a collar
or dog tag to show the new world
what you mean to me.

We're snowed in;
I could last until the sun
thaws us from the past
and frees us from this room.

Body Work

When people see the scars,
they flinch—I know it's hard to bear
staring at wrecked cars and shrapnel.

I can't bleach the ugly things
I've done, the bullet holes, the spray paint.
I can still smell the fumes on the tips of my fingers.

Once I scrape the rust from my body,
there is nothing but metal and marrow
left for the junkyard. I know it's hard

to rebuild a body from memory;
there are no instructions and nobody knows
how to connect the head to the heart.

PART TWO

HOW

TO

BUILD

A

HEART

Forgotten Love Songs
Mixed-Media Collage

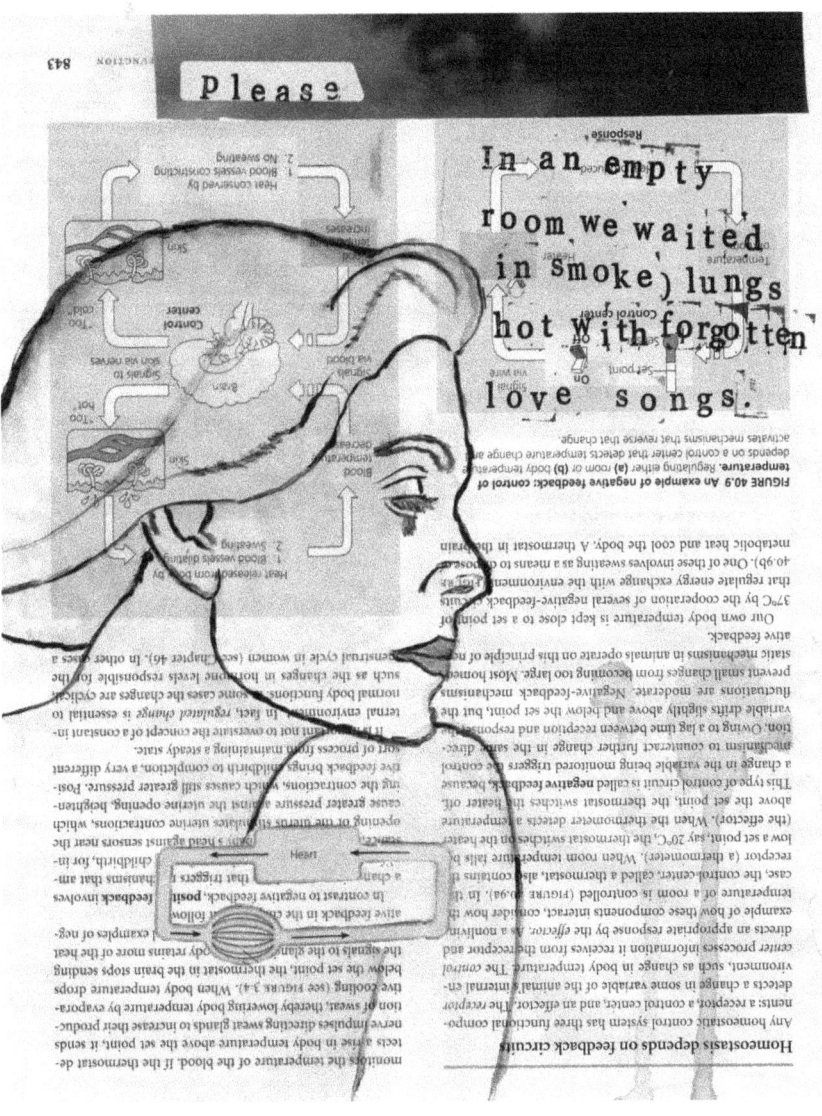

We Made Love and Dyed Your Hair Purple
Mixed-Media Collage

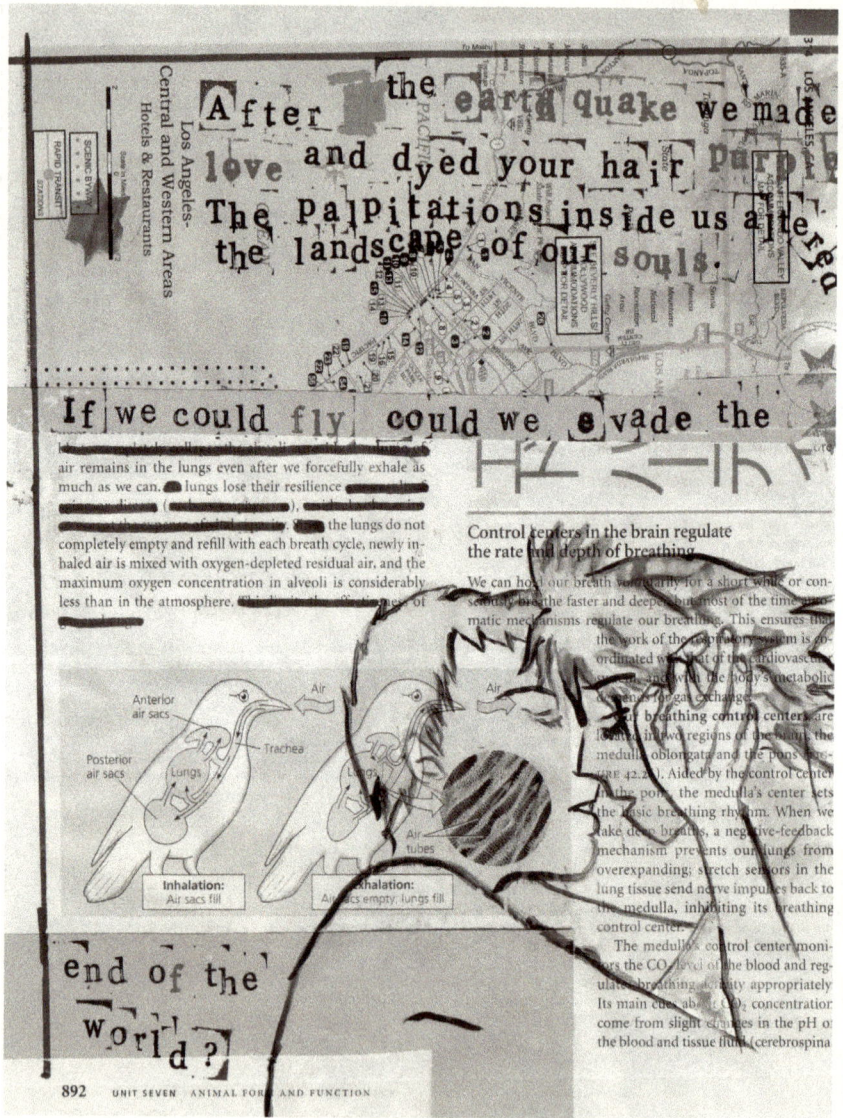

Flight of the Soul
Mixed-Media Collage

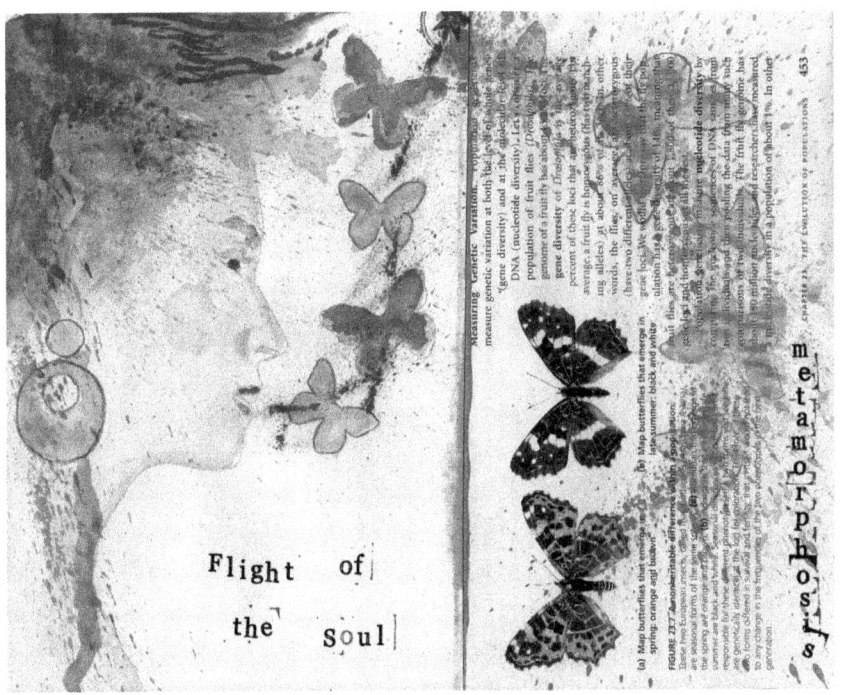

Sometime, Somewhere
Mixed-Media Collage

The Untamed Heart
Mixed-Media Collage

PART THREE

FROM

LOS

ANGELES

WITH

LOVE

Silver Halide

We tried to photograph our love
at the Venice Canals, those shallow
waterways leading to the dark sea.
As if we could capture a spark
in a jar, like a firefly. Eventually,
it would suffocate, like the photo,
not enough air to develop
the film of our history.

If our love played out at twenty-four
frames per second, the projectionist would need
to know about the third act, the burning
of the canals after we set fire
to the bridge between us.
One second and a smile
could never express the story
of a ship sinking
in shallow waters.

A Shallow Argument at Venice Beach

The Pacific begs me to swim away, anything
to keep us from strangling each other
on the boardwalk. The Freakshow

is where our love belongs, a two-headed
oddity feasting on dust and bone
until there is nothing left of us.

You sell watercolors of women's faces
and I write the words nobody wants
to remember. I want you to paint

me. You want me to write about us:
As the sun sets over the ocean,
I fade into your torn canvas.

Nobody knows we're fighting; even seagulls
refuse the scraps of our misery. We become debris,
swirling shreds of paper in the salty wind.

There Are Nights I Lie

naked in your bed, I hear the bathwater
rinse you of our make-up sex sweat, I smoke

your cigarettes, I look out your window, and I remember
a girl who loved me but moved to Boston and South Korea,

how I was too afraid to move away with her,
even after she bought me a ticket both times.

You look at me with a green eye and a grey one,
and I can't believe that you're going blind, no matter

how many times you say the doctors warn you. The heart sees
the truth even if the eyes cannot, but still the night

can be my excuse to hold you and imagine what Seoul
would feel like, and if it's as cold there as it is

in your arms. I fear even the friction of our bodies
will not save us from another winter of desperation.

Playing Your Old Guitar on the Fourth of July

It worked: you smiling, strumming
as you sang a verse, moving me

with those boney fingers picking thin strings,
calloused. You cautioned the wooden skeleton

in my hands, you said, *Just feel
its neck and body. Press the bronze down*

on the fret board, let the skin almost break.
It burned like your vacant touch

when the watercolor sky crescendoed.
I wondered if you understood the language

of light and fire and blood.
How else could you have known

the perfect tempo to play along
with the horizon? You alone

possessed a fluency of music
enough to interpret me.

if you want a revolution
    for levy

blow as hard as you can
until the molten glass changes

remember that form is everything

smoke as many cigarettes as Bette Davis
hold them like her too

then transform words into lassos
use them to pull down granite goddesses

never forget
you have a world to cover with fire

shatter light bulbs before you pray for illumination
ask yourself the question why was Ted Berrigan's
window full of darkness?
                      because when a poet strikes a match
                      it burns starlight

Blind Alto Midnight
for Clifford Murphy

Percussion landmines echo behind
the six-string war and drowning liquor
symphony—an armistice to cure starvation
for highs, quick fixes, hungry

hearts. This loud bass-line anthem
booms in the dusty downtown hollow.
The blues bellow a long way south, down
the calloused fret board and moan,

where the fingertips will die fighting
for a place to survive and electrocute jazz.
While widows quiver, whispering alto love
notes, amplifying the busy bar tone,

a fire climbs the vocal chimney to howl
one final chorus, a wicked verse, an acoustic
rhythm of dead melody hanging like airwaves
in the darkness of blind vibes.

As soft rain opens for thunder,
midnight harmonies pick phosphor bones
in sync with empty lightning shadows before
all souls exit their bodies in perfect sync.

The Cliffs of Palos Verdes

I've eaten from the nest,
buried bones enough to pick
my pale heart's flesh from the ocean's
coral teeth. What crow corpse weeps

without marring a lover in its wings?
A harbor night, turbulent foam beneath
our broken tree, we plumed
each other's feathers clean.

In the mirror of the hungry sea,
I fell and you reached, your talons
unable to defy gravity

or save this winged creature
who unlearned to fly.

Aboard the Sunset Limited

In this confined space we rediscover
how the heart travels with the body but always
seems to run in place. A renewal of vows,
because we must prove ourselves
to the ocean, lost hurricanes—

a lot like love stuffed into a sleeper car.
The desert welcomes us to the throat of El Paso,
where we swim to the gut and fly to the coast
with a wedding dress, broken champagne
glasses. In the wet heat you call home,

spouses drive into apartment buildings
with propane tanks as a sign of devotion.
We will reunite for waves until swept under,
the current a train we can't deboard. Ignore
the tide's pull, a vacuum—we must surrender

forty-eight hours together on the rail,
our testimonies written on paper, our ink
so heavy it bleeds the words we scratch
in the spare moments of stillness,
when our eyes fail to meet.

Nathan Elias is the author of the novelette *A Myriad of Roads That Lead to Here*. He grew up in Toledo, Ohio and moved to Los Angeles, California where he wrote, acted in, and directed films such as *The Chest*. Nathan holds an MFA in Creative Writing from Antioch University Los Angeles and currently lives in Tampa, Florida where he aspires to teach writing. Nathan's fiction, poetry, and films are available at www.Nathan-Elias.com